Mental Toughness for Young Athletes

Eight Proven 5-Minute Mind Exercises For Kids And Teens Who Play Competitive Sports!

Moses and Troy Horne

Want to go to the next level?

Visit Gamereadycourse.com to learn more!

Table of Contents

Introduction

Are You All in Or Nah?

It was 1997 and the Lakers were playing the Utah Jazz in Game 5 for the western conference title. Kobe Bryant was walking the ball up the floor during the last five seconds of the fifth game of the series. The Lakers were down in the series 1-3. This game was going to decide if the Lakers championship run would come to an end or not. Kobe crossed half court and with the shot clock ticking down past the five-second mark, the four-second mark, the three-second mark he shot the ball to try to win the game. It was an air ball!

KOBE SHOT AN AIR BALL ON LIVE TV IN A CHAMPIONSHIP GAME!

The ball didn't hit anything. "Air ball! Air ball!" the audience chanted. That air ball sent the game into overtime. The Laker's future still hung in the balance, but I am sure that Kobe was not concerned at all. He was the Mamba right? Well, during overtime "The Mamba" shot three more air balls for a total of four! One of them could have tied the game and saved the Lakers' season. At the end of the day, the Lakers lost that game and ended their season. Four air balls meant no championship that season. Keywords being . . . THAT

SEASON!

Jerry West, the Lakers general manager at the time, you know, the guy that's the NBA logo, went on to say this about Kobe's four air ball shots in their championship game.

> I believe most definitely that was a defining moment in his career. Do you know why? If somebody would have shot an air ball on our team and shot a second one, they ain't gonna shoot a third one. He was fearless. I think that's one of the things that spurred him to greatness. He wasn't going to allow himself to fail.

Jerry West almost got it right. You see, the thing that made Kobe fearless was that he WAS going to allow himself to fail.

If you don't get anything else from this book, get this. Instagram and TikTok only show the makes. Allow yourself to fail. Allow yourself to miss shots. Allow yourself to strike out. Allow yourself to miss tackles. Allow yourself to fail! That is the only way that you are going to succeed.

Who Is This Book For?

This book is for elite athletes in elementary school, middle school, and high school. Simple enough right? If you found yourself saying something like, "Elite elementary school athletes?" this book isn't for you. Actually, before I get too far into who this book is for let me tell you who this book is not for. You ought to know because you don't want to waste your time, or mine for that matter. Yeah . . . it's like that. Life is too short to read a book that isn't meant for you. So, let's all get on the same page from the beginning.

Who this book is NOT for?

- If you are looking for an easy mental toughness solution or an easy way to get fast results you have picked up the wrong book.

- If you don't like having difficult conversations to reach new levels of success this book is not for you.

- If it is more important for you to be cool with your boys or your girls then this book isn't for you.

Return this book or give it to someone who is ready and willing to do the hard work that it takes to become a mentally elite athlete. Look, I'm not trying to brag or anything, but I have talked with the Kobe Bryants, Chauncey Billups, Earl Boykins, Jason Richardsons, and the Coach Steve Smiths of the world. I've talked with former pros and current Division 1 players. This elite youth sports thing is not a path for kids who ain't willing to get after it. So, if you are not ready to go all in this book is not for you.

However, if you are:

- Ready to get your mind right.

- Ready to have some difficult conversations with yourself first and sometimes your teammates.

- Ready to listen to your mom or dad or whoever is reading the parent version of this book.

- Ready to fail in order to succeed.

Basically, if you are ready to do what it takes to be great and mentally tough, then this book is going to be a good fit for you! Move forward accordingly.

Your True Ride Or Dies

First off, your parents are on your side. Don't forget that. I get it. Sometimes they can be annoying as heck, but your parents are your true ride or dies. For you youngsters who don't know what "ride or die" means, it basically means that they are the ones that are going to be there no matter what. They will ride with you or die trying. So, rock with them like they got you because they got you. Everyone else should be a distant second. EVERYONE! Family on three. One, two three: FAMILY!

Second, they are going to get it wrong sometimes but that's part of the process. Look, this isn't school. It is real out here in these streets and yeah, your parents are going to get it wrong sometimes, but guess what. When they do, they are going to work like heck to make it right. Love him or hate him, LaVar Ball is a prime example of what I'm talking about. He took Melo out of High School so that he could play overseas. He didn't look into the paperwork correctly and his time in Lithuania made him not only ineligible for top-level high school games it also made him ineligible for college.

Where is Melo Ball now? He's one of the few basketball players in the world who gets to say that he plays in the NBA! He won the "Rookie of the Year" title and he currently plays for the Charlotte Hornets!

Many people don't know this, but did you know that Coach

John Lucas of John Lucas Enterprises and former #1 Draft Pick for the Houston Rockets called in every favor for his son John III that he could? I know this because he told me at his John Lucas Invitational Camp. It might not have had a direct effect, but John Lucas III did eventually end up playing for twelve years in the league.

Another little known fact is that Dell Curry fought for Steph, Joe went to bat for Kobe, and Richard Williams went to bat for Venus and Serena. Parents are your true ride or die. So, no matter how much you get annoyed by them, remember that they got your back and rock with them first and foremost.

Mental Confidence Is Inevitable With These Exercises

How am I so confident, you ask? I am confident because I use these exercises myself. Now I do have my own ups and downs with mental toughness, but these exercises always help me get back to where I'm supposed to be.

This book is going to be your mental toughness workout blueprint and I suggest you use it often. This is not a one-time thing. These exercises have been used by all of the top athletes, including 100% of the sports icons that you know and love.

I'm talking about Michael Jordan, Pelé, Venus and Serena Williams, Michael Phelps, Kobe Bryant, Missy Franklin, and lots of others. This stuff works! You just have to commit to the journey. Just because the exercises are five minutes long doesn't mean that the process will be. Mental toughness is a long process. This is not a "get-tough-quick" scheme. It took you years to get to where you are. It's going to take some time to move from where you are to the mentally tough you.

Give it that time. Be patient with yourself and the work that you will need to do to make this happen. As the saying goes . . .

Rome was not built in a day.

Make sure that you have the support around you that you need. Surround yourself with people who are committed to being better. If the people around you are not committed to being better, then surround yourself with new people. It's really that serious.

For those of you who live in small towns and don't have a lot of people or teams to choose from, surround yourself with your family. Remember, they are the ones who are going to be there through everything anyway. Also, there is a lot of YouTube information out there (basketball, football, volleyball, baseball, and any other sport you can think of). Watch it to learn more and get better. More on that later.

As someone who has been where you are, I can tell you that this mental toughness journey is 1000% worth everything that you are about to put into it. The mental toughness transition and growth that you are about to see in yourself is going to be awesome.

Our Results

Two minutes left in the game. Parents and coaches are all cheering and screaming. I come across half court and sink another three-pointer to put my team comfortably ahead. With that final shot, I achieved my first triple double.

Thanks to these mental toughness exercises, I was able to have a pretty good middle school basketball career. I went to camps like CP3 Middle School Combine which led me to CP3 Rising Stars. I also went to John Lucas camp in Los Angeles which then led to the John Lucas' Elite Invitational in Houston, Texas. I have been to a lot of camps with a lot of ranked kids and let me tell you that you need to have your mental toughness game on point.

Mental toughness is responsible for me being offered a varsity spot as an incoming freshman. Mental toughness made it possible for me to catch the attention of some of the top AAU teams in my state, top high school basketball coaches (even basketball prep school coaches), and even Division 1 college coaches. All this is happening to a 6'1 incoming high school freshman. Not bad if I do say so myself.

Mental toughness is amazing, and it works! This book is your mental toughness map. It will make the long trip seem a little shorter. This book will guide you past all of the wrong turns and needless detours that you might have taken.

Now, before you get all excited, I should warn you about some of the problems and roadblocks that you are going to face along the way. You need to know what's coming. Because, if you are not ready for the roadblocks that are going to try to trip you up, you could find yourself back where you started! Unfortunately, I speak from experience. You don't want those avoidable setbacks right now. So, I'm going to tell you what to look out for.

The 3 Major Mental Toughness Roadblocks

Here are the top three mental toughness roadblocks that almost every athlete struggled with when they were working on their mental toughness.

Roadblock #1 – Current Beliefs. Good or bad, you are performing at the level you are because, in some part of you, you believe that's how good you are. Right now, you see yourself exactly like you are showing up. If you want to be mentally tough you have to see yourself as mentally tough. I am going to give you the mental exercises that the pros have used to help themselves do just that.

Roadblock #2 – Peers. "If nine of your friends are broke you will be number 10." – Steve Harvey. Like it or not, you become part of what you are around. If the people that you allow yourself to be surrounded by are not mentally tough (or not working on it), then you will not be mentally tough. A successful road to mental toughness cannot include friends who are not on the same page.

Roadblock #3 – Other Authority Figures. Take responsibility for this one too. Because you have been showing up a certain way, your teachers or coaches now perceive you in a certain way. It's going to be hard to change their minds. Also, if the adults around you are filled with the "you can't do this" and the "that's unrealistic" mentality, be respectfully disconnected. Your career is on the line. You have your true ride or dies with you. What else do you need? Keep your head up and keep working. They'll catch up.

It Wasn't All Sunshine And Rainbows – Our Struggle

There were a lot of setbacks. I lost full seasons because I didn't understand some of the things I am going to share with you. I have experienced the mental challenges that take place when someone tells you that you are a practice player. I have endured the game after game long car rides where you just can't find happiness in the only sport that you love. I have even wondered if this elite sports thing is for me or if it's time to quit. Everybody wonders that.

Muhammad Ali wondered it when he fought Joe Frazier the third time. Floyd Mayweather has said he's had moments of doubt where he asked himself if boxing was for him. A lot of elite athletes ask themselves these questions when they get challenged. You're not the only one who wonders, but you are the only one who can answer that question for you.

For me, basketball is it. I'm in this for life. I can't know that for you. You have to decide that for yourself. However, if you do decide that you are into your sport for life, then you better go all in. There are too few slots available and too many young athletes to do anything else.

Having a mental toughness regime has changed all of that for me. I was really lucky. I got to talk directly with mental toughness giants like Chauncey Billups, Earl Boykins, Jason Richardson, and KOBE BRYANT! You can listen to those interviews on my free podcast called *Hoopchalk* if you would like. Hearing it straight from them is a gift that I don't take for granted.

Imagine being able to get the keys to the Mamba mentality straight from the Mamba himself at thirteen years old. That was me! Because of that mental training, I now know how to conquer performance anxiety when it arises, and I know what work to do whenever I experience mental setbacks. In this book, I am going to share all of the stuff that I learned with you.

Finally, before we get into the "how-tos," let's take one final moment to help you dispel the myths that come with mental training.

Mental Toughness Myths of Destruction

I know that right now many of you are probably thinking "Moses! Enough with the warm-ups. Let's get into the mental toughness workout!" But, just like a physical workout, your warm-up is super important. A proper warm-up will keep you from getting injured and this book is a workout for your mind, guys! Take the time to get in the right frame of mind so that you can make the most of this information. You're in this for the journey, my friend. Trust the process. Commit to the time it takes to warm up so that you don't injure your brain! Ha! Ok, now onward to our final warm-up exercise. Let's do some myth-busting!

Myth #1 – Born With It. Like many things in sports, a lot of people believe you just have to be born with "it," (whatever "it" is). Let me just say that every sports icon that I have talked to says the complete opposite. Chauncey said that when he was a kid he decided to focus on basketball because he knew that it would give him the best chance to succeed. Kobe said that for one full summer he didn't score one point because he was horrible. Every person that I talked to said that they worked more than most. None of them said, "I was just born with natural talent." Most people believe that mental toughness is a naturally inherited skill that you either have or you don't.

You're either a dawg or you're not. That is a myth. Just ask the pros yourself. Learn their stories and pay attention to how many of them say they made a choice to put in the work nobody else was willing to do. There is no "born with it" gene. There is only a "worked for it" gene.

Mental toughness is no different. You have to choose to become mentally tough. Don't believe me? Take a listen to Kobe "Black Mamba" Bryant say it himself.

In our interview with him (Yes! As I said before, I interviewed FREAKIN' KOBE BRYANT!) he talked about his books *The Wizenard Series*. He said that he wrote the character Twig after himself. Twig is the quiet kid from a middle-class family who had to learn to find his mental toughness, his voice, and his role on the team. Sound familiar?

Hearing that even the Mamba wasn't born with the Mamba mentality should be enough to let you know that mental toughness is an attainable skill. Visit gamereadycourse.com to hear the Mamba himself share with us some of his own mental toughness tips.

Myth #2 – They'll Figure It Out. The expression "they

have to figure it out by themselves" is one of the craziest sayings that I have ever heard. IMO Dell Curry helped Steph "figure it out." Richard Williams helped Venus and Serena "figure It Out." If you think that Missy Franklin just showed up to the pool every day and coached herself, you are dreaming. Listen, I get it, sometimes our parents and coaches can be annoying, but they have more experience than we do. We should listen to them.

Yeah, I know they can get on your nerves, but at the end of the day, they have twenty, thirty, and in some cases forty more years of experience than you do. You might want to listen to them. (For now.) Think about it this way. If your little brother or sister were to come to you and ask you how to do better in kindergarten, would you tell them? Also, if you started to tell them what to expect in kindergarten and they started arguing with you, wouldn't you be a little annoyed? "Bro! You have never been to kindergarten. I have! You might want to listen." Well, that's your relationship with your parents right now.

It won't always be this way, but for right now your job is to let them help you figure it out. Don't try to do this alone if you don't have to. Encourage them to get the parent version of this book if they don't have it. This youth sports journey is going to be a dog fight. You need their help.

I have been to a bunch of elite camps and let me tell you that all of the parents of "ranked" or "elite athletes" are guiding their kids and their kids are listening to them. They are clearly not leaving it 100% up to the kid and the kids aren't trying to do it by themselves. Follow their lead!

Myth #3 – Mental Toughness Training Doesn't Work. Guys! LeBron James just came out with his own mental training app called Calm. Aaron Gordon had one before him and Michael Jordan, Kobe Bryant, and countless other professional athletes have paid a guy named George Mumford a lot of money to help them with their mental toughness. Studies have shown that the mind controls 90 plus percent of our reality. If they are paying to have people train them on mental toughness you might want to try it.

Henry Ford said, "Whether you think you can or think you can't. You're right."

Albert Einstein, one of the smartest people to ever spend time on planet earth said, "Your imagination is your preview of life's coming attractions."

Mental toughness training has produced sports giant after sports giant, as you will see in this book. Don't allow yourself to spend one more second in the world of old, outdated thinking. These sports pros have shown that mental training is super important. Listen to them.

Fun Fact: Did you know that pretty much every college and professional sports team these days has a team sports psychologist? Their goal is to help their athletes decode this mental training performance thing. Start now and you will be ahead of everyone else. Don't leave it to chance.

Last But Not Least – Fixed Mindset vs. Growth Mindset

Confidence, anxiety, and a lack of mental toughness are not fixed. You can work on them. Remember, all of the pros that I talked to said that they worked for everything! That means that at one point they were not good! Heck, Kobe even said that when he was eleven or twelve he was HORRIBLE. These problems are actually pretty common among young athletes. Our struggles with confidence and excessive anxiety often leads to young talented athletes quitting the sport they love. We often start sports super excited to be like our idols! And then we let one game or one coach or one mistake ruin our love for the game.

But you don't have to be a casualty of the mental game. You can be a winner of the mental game. I truly believe that if the young athletes who gave up on their sports dreams had been taught mental toughness, they would have overcome their doubts and fears. I know it's a bold statement, but I think that it's 100% true. Here's what Kobe said to me when we talked about how to get better.

"Learn the basics and do them over and over and over and over and over again."- Kobe Bryant

He said he wasn't the most athletic. He said that the other kids were better than him, but he knew that if he just worked on one thing at a time until he perfected it he was going to eventually catch them and pass them. In his words, it's just math.

Top athletes know that just one game cannot and does not define their career or their abilities. They know that one shot, whether made or missed, does not determine who they are or how they will play in the future. They all know that ALL of their games will determine that. They've learned how to keep away anxiety and low confidence by working more than everyone else, and that is why they are at the top of the sports world. My dad always tells me when I make a shot or miss a shot, "It's not hot or cold. It's just math."

What he means is, if you are a 40% shooter in practice and you miss six shots in a row, the next four are going in. Trust yourself and your work even when nobody else does. If you shoot four air balls, then get back in the gym after the game. That's what Kobe did. Right after his four air ball game, nineteen-year-old Kobe didn't go home and play video games. He went to the gym. Be like Kobe! It's not hot or cold, it's just math. Kobe understood that.

Also, at the end of the day, remember that basketball, football, baseball, soccer, volleyball, or whatever sport you play is just a game. It's just a shot. It's just a run. It's just a tackle. Make or miss, it's just a shot. Don't make the moment bigger than it is. Now let's get to the hard work. Roll up your sleeves, my friend. I think you are ready.

"It's About To Go Down"

– Kevin Hart

Chapter 1:
Your Ride Or Die And You–
Family Culture

Decide that you are going to win. It all begins with a mindset. Will Smith said:

"Make a choice, decide, and focus on what it's going to be, who you're going to be, how you're going to do it!" – *Will Smith*

Before you do any of that, you have to first decide that you are going to be successful. Before you can be, have, or do anything on or off of the court, you have to decide what "it" is. As Mark Twain once said…

"I can teach anybody how to get what they want out of life. The problem is that I can't find anybody who can tell me what they want." – *Mark Twain*

No matter what IT is, you and your parent or coach have to decide that you are going to have "it." You have to decide that you are going to achieve your goals. You have to decide that you are going to win no matter how crazy your dreams may sound to other people. You have to believe in your vision. You have to get rid of your fears and limiting beliefs. You have to decide that you are going to win. Sometimes your parents are going to doubt and sometimes they are going to help you fight off your doubts. But no matter what, you have to be the champion of your dreams.

You have to decide what your goals are and you have to believe that you will reach them.

Imagine the level of belief Venus and Serena Williams had to have to believe that they were going to be the greatest tennis players who ever played the game.

1. Their father and coach at the time had never played tennis.

2. They lived in COMPTON, California.

3. They had no money.

4. Plus, all of their friends probably thought that they were crazy!

Belief is super important. Despite what other people think you have to tell yourself every day that you are going to be what you want to be. EVERY DAY!

Can you imagine the Williams family working together with the aim of being the best in tennis on those broken down courts in Compton back in the late 80s and early 90s? I think Serena said she remembers hearing gunshots all of the time. Look, no matter how tough you think it is for you, your mind can get you to any goal. Your belief has to be like the Williams family.

Once you decide that, no matter what people say is "realistic," you are going to achieve your goal, then the rest is easy. Once you decide that you are going to believe in yourself, the rest is inevitable!

"I'm the greatest! I said it BEFORE I knew I was" – **Muhammad Ali**

Adopt and Adapt

Don't wait for everything to be perfect. A lot of us make the mistake of believing that we need the perfect conditions to play well. We want to be inside the perfect gym. We think that we have to have the perfect shoes. We think that the net has to be in a certain way. Those things have nothing to do with anything. You have to learn that the imperfections are additional training obstacles to overcome. When obstacles happen, they are there to help you get better. Over at gamereadycourse.com I put together some videos for you to see what I mean. Go check it out if you can. They will help a lot.

If you are struggling for playing time you just have to commit to working your way up. Always offer to guard the best player whether you get beat all of the time or not. When you do this, you are getting better. I know a guy who used to play against Donovan Mitchell. He said that in high school Donovan Mitchell was a walking bucket, and not in a good way. What he meant was that any time he had Donovan on him he knew that he was going to get a bucket. Today Donovan is in the NBA. My friend is not. It's a long journey. Keep working and celebrate when things are hard. They are helping you get better.

In baseball, Mark Buehrle was cut from his high school baseball team, but he went on to be the most consistent pitcher in baseball history. Michael Jordan was cut from his high school team and, as we all know, he went on to become one of the greatest to ever play the game.

The one thing that's going to help you the most is being honest with yourself. You have to approach your truth-telling from a growth mindset perspective, not a fixed mindset perspective. A growth mindset says that wherever you are right now is only temporary. If you suck, you won't suck forever. If you work at anything you can change it. Approach everything with this growth mindset.

Remember that Steph Curry rebuilt his shot in high school. For a full summer, he didn't shoot outside of the arc. Steph didn't have any offers to play college basketball until late in his senior season. Mike Piazza was the 1,390th player of the 62nd round. I didn't even know they picked that many people in the MLB!

Each of these athletes went all in on who they were, and it worked out for the better. They were honest with themselves and kept working.

Kobe told us that the secret, that isn't really a secret, is hard work. You have to be willing to work more than everyone else. Do that and the rest will take care of itself. Look at the story of Desi Linden in the 2018 Boston Marathon. On the day of her record-setting marathon run, the weather was unusually cold, windy, and wet. It wasn't a good day for running. She is even quoted saying, "My hands were freezing, and there are times where you were just stood up by the wind. It was comical how slow you were going, and how far you still had to go."

"At six miles I was thinking, 'No way, this is not my day,'" Linden said. "Then you break the tape and you're like, 'This is not what I expected today.'" Her training took over and she became the first U.S. runner to win the event in 33 years. Without the hard work, she would have lost the race that made her the first American woman to win the Boston Marathon since Larsen Weidenbach in 1985.

You have to be willing to adjust and adapt. The best way to do that is to work harder. The best way to work harder is to make your practice more difficult than the game or competition. If you are doing it right the game will feel easy.

Stay Focused

Most kids hate the practice of staying focused. But the greats all say that at some point they had to find their focus to become great. Being mentally tough will require you to focus.

In the book *Outliers,* Malcolm Gladwell talked about the 10,000-hour rule. The rule says that most of the people who went on to dominate in their sport had practiced their craft for approximately 10,000 hours. Anders Ericsson came along and wrote that it needed to be 10,000 hours of what he calls "deliberate practice." That means that you not only need to work on a skill for 10,000 hours, you also need to be very specific about what you are doing when you practice. You have to be focused.

Learn From Failure

The problem with failure is that we think there is a problem with failure. Failure is a gift, and when you help change your thoughts around failure it changes your perception of the outcome. When you learn to celebrate failure, you will find yourself winning more.

Every successful person tells everyone who will listen that their greatest gift was learning to fail. They had to learn to fail often, fail forward, and fail fast.

You have to take a lot of chances. You have to take a lot of swings, miss a lot of shots, and make a lot of mistakes. You have to look for situations that will allow you to fail. Avoid situations that demand perfection. Failure is great! It helps you learn what not to do.

Even the biggest stars lose big games. They know that it is part of the game. Failure is a part of their journey to success. I have some videos for you to watch over at gamereadycourse.com. They are basically videos of greats saying the same thing, just in case you need more proof. Go to gamereadycourse.com and get your free download. Here are some other quotes that I think might help you seek out failure.

Thomas Edison said this about his light bulb invention: *"I have not failed 1,000 times. I've just found 10,000 ways that won't work."*

Sanya Richards-Ross said that trying and failing was more honorable than not trying when she said, *"Failure I can live with. Not trying is what I can't handle."*

Michael Jordan said, *"I can accept failure; everyone fails at something. But I can't accept not trying."*

Wayne Gretzky said, *"You miss 100% of the shots you don't take."*

Nastia Liukin hit the nail on the head when she said, *"If you're afraid of failure, you don't deserve success."*

Serena Williams wrapped it all up in a neat little bow by saying, *"If anything, you know, I think losing makes me even more motivated."*

The More You Fail, The More You Will Succeed

The real failure is when you decide to stay down when you get knocked down. Don't believe me? Here are some more people who discovered who they were and then committed to being true to themselves above everything else. Being true to yourself, never giving up when you fail, working hard, and celebrating failure is super important when it comes to being successful. Take a look!

Steve Jobs (Founder of Apple) – dropped out of college, his first computer barely sold, he was later removed from his own company, then he went on to build the first trillion-dollar company in the history of mankind.

Oprah Winfrey – demoted as a news reporter, deemed "unfit for television," then went on to find such great success on the screen and in the world of business that today she's worth $3.5 billion.

Michael Jordan – cut from his basketball high school team, missed more shots than most of the people to ever play the game of basketball (except Kareem Abdul-Jabbar), and went on to be the fifth-leading scorer in NBA history.

Failure is a part of the road to success. Do you know who holds the title of all-time leading scorer in NBA history? Kareem Abdul-Jabbar holds it. Do you know what he also holds? Mr. Abdul-Jabbar also holds the record for the most missed shots in NBA history. The greatest basketball player of all time is also the one who failed the most.

Failure is a necessary part of success. Learn to seek it out! Learn to celebrate it. Failure is learning all of the things that won't work. The more you fail, the closer you get to success.

Always Be Proactive

You are responsible for your success. Take responsibility for all of your actions and choices on and off the court. Take responsibility for your failures, but most importantly, take responsibility for your success, too.

People often get this wrong. They tell us to take responsibility when things go wrong, but then they tell us to give up responsibility to others when things go right. Now I'm not telling you not to thank others when things go well. However, I am telling you to thank yourself too when things go right. Got a video of Snoop Dog showing you how it's done over on the download. Go and check it out.

If you don't get anything else from this book get this: take responsibility for EVERYTHING. The coach sat you down? Take responsibility for being "sit downable." What can you do to change that in the future? You didn't play as well as you thought you should have. What can you work on in practice to make your in-game performance better? Be proactive when it comes to your journey. Make your journey a journey that depends very little on outside favors or outside influence.

The best way to do this is to work hard, love failure, and put yourself in a position to succeed. And, of course, take responsibility for everything. Here's how to do that with confidence.

Do Your Research. Instead of looking at the opinions of everybody else, look at their results. Do your research! Don't look at what people say; look at what people do instead. Look at the outcomes of their actions. If their results are the results that you want, then follow their advice. If they aren't, don't! It's really that simple.

With the internet, you can follow pretty much any sports icon's journey and do what they did.

1. You can see where they practice.
2. You can see what they work on.
3. You can see what teams they play for.
4. You can see how they train and who they train with.
5. You can learn more now than you could've ever learned about their process.
6. So, LEARN IT!
7. Use the internet! Find someone who is just a few years ahead of you and follow their path. Copy their journey. That's what Kobe did! It looks like it worked out for him.

Once You've Done The Research, follow Your Gut! Trust yourself! Right or wrong, trust yourself and your parents to make the best moves for your career. When you do the research, you will become what Malcolm Gladwell calls an "Outlier." You want that!

A basketball coach once told me at CP3 camp, "You are a great player, but you are too nice." He told me that basketball is a lonely journey. You will spend more time by yourself than you will with a group of people that are all on the same page. I'm not telling you to become anti-social, but I am telling you to find more comfort in being around like-minded people. Doing that will limit the number of people that you will be able to associate with consistently, but that is part of the game.

When was the last time that you saw your favorite sports star in a group photo with all of her friends at the mall or a party? Exactly! Most people aren't going to like this part, but the greats aren't like most people. They don't do what most people do. You have to decide if you are going to be like the elite or like most people. Are you going to take the path of the 99% or the 1%? Lastly, remember that your true ride or dies live under the same roof that you wake up under every morning. Family on three!

Your friends may turn on you, and it might lead to confidence-testing moments when you feel like you are wrong. Many of the opinions you hear will make you question your research. Don't do that. Don't question your facts-based research. Follow your gut.

I'm not saying that you won't have unsure moments throughout this journey. I am not saying that you won't fail. I am saying that even when you fail, and you will fail, you should remember that failure is good. Follow your gut; it will never lead you in the wrong direction. Remember, you are reacting internally to your research and knowledge. They are reacting to their feelings and opinions. Facts always win.

Chapter Summary

- Have a winning mentality.

- Stay focused.

- Your failure will make you succeed.

- Always trust yourself and follow your gut.

Well, congratulations! You did it! You made it to the end of chapter 1. I know that usually is not celebrated in books, but this ain't no ordinary book and you ain't no ordinary person, so take a minute and celebrate your first achievement. Going forward, set small attainable goals on your journey toward your big goal and celebrate the heck out of them when you reach them. As Norman Vincent Peale said,

*"By the yard it's hard, but inch by inch everything is a sinch!" – **Norman Vincent Peale***

YEAH YOU! Nice work. True story: most people don't make it to the end of the first chapter in many of the books that they buy, and you have! You are different. You are exceptional! I just wanted to take a moment to celebrate that with you.

At the end of each chapter, I am going to share a book that

helped me with reaching the goal of the chapter. This chapter's book is *Mindset* by Carol Dweck. If you haven't read it, read it!

Here is the first book that I suggest you read yourself or share with your young athlete:

Listen To *Mindset* by Carol Dweck

For a complete list of books and resources go to gamereadycourse.com/

Chapter 2:
How To Strengthen Your Subconscious Mind! – Exercise #1

Your subconscious mind controls everything that you do without you even realizing it. That means that when you reprogram your subconscious mind in the right way, you will do the things you need to do to be great without having to give it much thought. Remember the story about Desi Linden the marathon runner? She won that race because, before the race, she had reprogrammed her subconscious mind. If you have ever run for long distances, you know what I am talking about. After the first mile or so your body is on autopilot and it is basically running by itself.

Your subconscious mind is the foundation of everything that we will be doing in this book. That is why we have to start with it. Your subconscious mind will build your confidence and help you with those split-second decisions that come up on the court or the field. Your subconscious mind will decide to shoot or not to shoot. Coaches are looking for a person who wants to take the shot when it matters most. Preparing your subconscious mind will help you be that person.

Your subconscious is your storage space because it keeps records of every outcome, good or bad. It saves it for when the same situation happens again. It only takes one time to get burned by fire for you to know to be careful around a flame next time you see one. That is your subconscious mind at work.

The problem that most of us have is that we treat every situation or failure like getting burned. Failures, like being burned by a fire, are supposed to be treated differently than, say, striking out or missing a volley or missing a tackle. Don't treat all failures the same. Some are for learning and repeating until you reach success. Treat every failure like it's supposed to be treated. Learn to see failures differently than sports mistake failures. They are not the same.

Your subconscious mind has been keeping track of everything since you were born. It is the ultimate supercomputer with super terabyte storage. Have you ever been on the field during a game and just performed a skill on autopilot? That was a skill your subconscious mind safely stored for you from your many hours of practice.

Most athletes haven't been taught to use their subconscious mind, so during high-pressure in-game moments they turn to their conscious mind. This is why they fail.

Have you ever tried to do moves during the game that you have never practiced? That is you turning to your conscious mind for help. When this happens, and sometimes it will, that is your cue that you need to develop your subconscious mind more. You do that by doing more hard work. Four air balls in a championship game on national TV = Get back in the gym. Take it from Kobe. Video over at gamereadycourse.com

Understanding The Language Of Your Subconscious Mind

Ok, so now you know that your subconscious mind basically controls 97% percent of your life. You don't think about telling your heart to beat. Your subconscious mind does that for you. You don't think about breathing in and breathing out. Your subconscious mind does that for you too. Your subconscious mind basically lives for you and it does it automatically. When you walk down the street you don't think "left foot, right foot, left foot...?" Your subconscious mind does that for you. Your subconscious mind runs your world, so let's make it run the way you want.

Now here is the catch. Your subconscious mind has no filter. Your subconscious mind can't tell your positive thoughts from your negative thoughts. It's working too hard to keep you alive. It just accepts everything you feed it, so be careful what you tell it. Everything that you say goes straight into your subconscious mind with no filter. I will show you what I mean here in a few minutes, but always remember that your subconscious mind is an open book. Mentally tough people surround themselves with the reality that they want to see. They make sure that they don't allow their subconscious mind to hear anything that they don't want to be their future reality.

Richard Williams was a master at this for his daughters. In the book *Venus and Serena Williams: A Biography*, Jacqueline Edmondson wrote about how Richard Williams would post signs around the tennis court that would remind Venus and Serena's subconscious minds of their goals. The signs would say things like:

"Venus, you must take control of your future." And "Serena, you must learn to use more topspin on the ball."

Both girls kept note cards courtside with similar reminders. Here's the beautiful part—their subconscious minds heard every word.

Venus took control of her future.

Serena started using more topspin on the ball.

They both became two of the greatest tennis players to ever play the game. It worked!

Here's another thing that you should be aware of. Your subconscious mind can't hear the word "don't." Your subconscious mind can't hear the word "do." Your subconscious mind only hears the noun and the instruction. Let me explain this to you with a little game. Follow my instructions.

1. Don't think about pizza.

2. What's the first thing that you are thinking about right now? We both know the answer is pizza.

3. Don't think about your shoes.

4. What's the first thing that you are thinking about now?

5. Don't think about a pink elephant.

6. Isn't this pretty crazy?

What was the first thing that you did when I gave you those instructions? The first thing that you did was think about exactly what I told you *not* to think about. That is your subconscious mind at work. Here's how you make it work for you.

Making Your Subconscious Mind Work For You

I am going to try to make this as easy as possible.

Step 1: Practice saying only what you want to be your reality. Stay away from phrases like "Don't miss" or "Don't swing at that." Remember you are talking to a mind that doesn't hear "don't." Your subconscious mind is hearing "Miss!" and "Swing at that!" You have to rephrase your words to say what you want to see.

Only tell your subconscious mind what you want to be your reality. Your subconscious mind is listening. Remember Richard Williams told his girls that he wanted their reality to be that of the greatest tennis stars to ever play the game.

Once you have decided what it's going to be, your job is to protect and grow your mind into a mind that will support your new reality.

Guard Your Thoughts

For you to be mentally tough, you have to be tough about the things you think about. You cannot allow any thought that isn't what you want to see to enter into your subconscious thought. Tell yourself that "You are the greatest!" or that "You can do this!" Tell yourself that every day, like

Muhammad Ali did. If you are not careful, others will try to plant negative thoughts that can neutralize all you've told yourself.

No matter how many positive thoughts you put in your mind, you will struggle when you allow other people to put negative thoughts in your mind. Stop entertaining thoughts like "I can't do it," or "I'm not cut out for this." Negative thoughts should not be allowed to enter your subconscious mind. No matter what, you must keep the mindset of a winner and a champion.

There is a famous video of Richard Williams defending the mind of Venus Williams when she was a kid. I put a link to the video over on the download or you can just Google "Richard Williams defends 14-year-old Venus" to see it for yourself. Watch him. Watch his determination. Watch how important he feels it is to defend her mind. That is the position that you must take to defend your mind.

This is not a game. This is your life. Take it seriously and take responsibility.

There is a story of a young athlete who was starting her basketball career. As part of her training routine, her coach required that she run laps around the court. When she finished the first round of running, she was exhausted. Her coach asked her what was going on in her head as she was running. She said that she was thinking how she hated running and that she felt like stopping.

Her coach told her to replace that negative thought with "I love running, and my body is strong." The result was that she ran around the field and finished with a smile. She rushed to her coach after her run and told her that she didn't realize that what she thought made any difference in how she felt and what she did.

Most of us are like this young athlete. We don't know what we don't know. But now that you know this, you must use this information to improve your life. In the words of Shia LaBeouf, "Do IT!"

Never Doubt Yourself Because Of Other People's Fears Or Failures

We both know that before professional athletes decided to go into their chosen sport, there were people who had tried and failed at that same sport. For some reason, adult people will be quick to tell us how difficult the sport is. Some adults will say things like, "It's very difficult to get go pro." Some of your friends will tell you how hard it is to make the school sports team, the college sports team, or a professional sports team. As crazy as it sounds, you have to learn to protect your mind from adults and negative friends. Never allow yourself to doubt you because of the fears or failures of others.

The thing you must remember when people try to put doubts in your mind is that their fears and doubts are not about you. Don Miguel Ruiz says in his book *The Four Agreements*, don't take anything personally. Never take or make anything a personal matter. Nothing is ever personal unless we make it personal.

Going forward remember: don't make it personal. Other people's fears, doubts, and failures have nothing to do with you. If anyone starts trying to feed your mind with negative talk, it is your responsibility to go all Richard Williams on that thought or that way of thinking. You owe you!

Use Your Subconscious Mind To Overcome Performance Anxiety

Sweaty palms, pounding heartbeats, racing thoughts, or even dizziness. If you have had any of these pregame jitters you gotta know that these feelings are gifts when you learn how to use them.

In the audio program Maverick Mindset (which I recommend at the end of this chapter), Dr. Eliot tells a story about how Bill Russell would throw up before every game because of his nerves. He learned how to harness his nervous energy.

You have to learn how to use the jitters for your good. Those nerves mean that you have a heightened awareness of what is going on. Use that energy to swing harder, jump higher, run faster. Use it to help you win.

In his audio program, Dr. Eliot talks about how in his final season Bill Russell was having a not-so-good year. He also tells us about how, despite him having a bad year, his team had hobbled their way into the NBA championship. The papers were having a field day on how the great Bill Russell was washed up. They were talking about how he should have retired last year and all of the things that newspapers say about people.

However, in his last game with the championship on the line, Bill Russell had to run into the bathroom to throw up.

His nerves had returned. In Dr. Eliot's story about the event, after throwing up, Bill Russell kicked down the door of the bathroom stall and said, "Don't worry guys! We are going to win!"

They won!

Your nerves are good. Use them and the power of your subconscious mind to win.

In the next chapter, we are going to talk about getting in the "zone." Using the exercise in the next chapter will help you achieve your best performance in the games that you play. In the next chapter, we will go over how to teach the subconscious mind exactly what you want it to learn. In the next chapter, we are going to go over how you can teach your subconscious mind to take over. It is not as difficult as you think once you learn how and practice the technique. So let's start practicing.

The Five-Minute Subconscious Mind Exercise For This Chapter

Here is a little exercise to get your subconscious mind in the right space. For five minutes every day, go through what you said to yourself that day. Go through all of it. Make sure that going forward, you only tell yourself what you want to be your reality. Remove anything that uses the word "don't" and increase the times that you tell yourself what you want to see in your future. No limits.

Remember, Richard told Venus and Serena that they were going to be great tennis players when they were kids living in

Compton.

Your subconscious mind is a BEAST! Use it for your good!

Chapter Summary

- The subconscious mind accepts what you tell it; it is a judge-free zone.

- The subconscious mind has no filter, you need to be careful about what you feed it.

- Make your subconscious mind work for you.

- Practice the five-minute subconscious mind exercise every day.

Here is a great book that I suggest you read.

The book for this chapter is: *The Four Agreements* by Don Miguel Ruiz. This book is a great one for your mindset journey. This is one that you want to read.

You should also listen to The Maverick Mindset by Dr. John Eliot. It's GREAT!

This book is a great book for life! It's also a great book for your mindset journey. This is one that you want to read.

For a complete list of books and resources go to

gamereadycourse.com/

Chapter 3:
The Visualization Workout – Exercise #2

Did you know that the Olympics that you and I watch on TV or from the stadium stands are the second version of the events? It's the second version at least to the Olympians. The first version of the Olympic events happens in the minds of the athletes. Most if not all of the athletes are using visualization before they approach their event. Olympic athletes visualize everything from the national anthems to the cheering crowds to the medal award ceremonies. They live every single moment in their head.

Do you remember Olympian Missy Franklin, the swimmer who won four gold medals at the London Olympic Games? She said that she uses visualization to picture everything that might happen. Missy said that she does a replay of her visualization "a million times" in her head so that she won't have to worry about anything when the race comes. She solves every possible problem in her mind and she wins every race in her head before she steps up to the blocks.

Another example is the judo star, Kayla Harrison, holder of an Olympic judo title. She said that before she went on to win her judo title, she was visualizing it every night before going to bed.

So many elite athletes are doing this, but I bet you have never heard of a young athlete or youth coach suggesting it to his or her team. Why not? Talent alone obviously isn't enough to make it to the elite level. You need mental toughness. You need visualization. Thanks to year-round sports, personal trainers, YouTube videos (more on that in a later chapter), and more, young athletes are almost as talented as some pros used to be on draft day twenty years ago.

Mental exercises are what give elite athletes an edge. Because of that, most professionals are actively honing their mental game. In the professional realm, sports coaches and psychologists are actively advocating for mental exercises for better performance. It's time to bring it to the youth sports world.

What Is Visualization?

Visualization is the exercise of seeing things in your mind before they happen. It is a process of creating a mental YouTube video of what you want to happen before it happens. Basically, it's a way to tell your subconscious mind what you want to happen before you step into the room or onto the court.

Football great, Pelé, used visualization religiously before every match. Notice that I didn't say *some* matches or the *important* matches. Pelé visualized before EVERY match. He said that he would come to the soccer pitch early to walk around it. He would breathe in the air. He would feel the ground under his feet. He would walk through the stands. He did this to make sure that his visualizations were vivid and detailed based on the arena.

After doing his visualization walk, he would go to the locker room, lie down, and play the game in its entirety in his mind. He would see himself scoring. He would see himself defending successfully. He would see himself as a success. Pelé found this to be just as important as practicing. In fact, it was a part of his practice. If it worked for Pelé, you might want to give it a try.

Coach Bob Bowman has been vocal about how he has used visualization to bring a swimmer that he coached twenty-two medals, eighteen of which are gold. Do you know who I'm talking about? This swimmer is no other than Michael Phelps. Bob Bowman has coached Phelps since his teenage years.

Bowman was interviewed once and told the interviewer about how Michael Phelps always watches the "mental tape" of his races before going to bed every night and then watches them again in the morning, visualizing winning a race from the whistle to the celebration.

The Great Thing About Visualization Is?

The great thing about visualization is that it is pretty easy to do. The difficult thing about visualization is that it is pretty easy to do. The problem is that most young athletes don't do it. The main thing you have to realize is that your subconscious mind doesn't know the difference between what is real or what is imagined. The subconscious mind sees your imagination and visualization as something just as real as what we call reality. That's pretty crazy if you think about it.

Visualizing allows you to have successful experiences over and over again. All you have to do is use your imagination. Visualization works because it's feeding your subconscious mind the images, ideas, and experiences that you want to experience. And, since your subconscious mind can't tell the difference, this imagination practice will empower your subconscious mind and bring your imagined vision into your conscious reality.

Visualization will not only increase your mental toughness, it will also eventually relieve most of your anxiety and stress in the game. Remember you want to keep the rest of it. Don't believe me? Check out this video that Cus D'Amato made about fear. It's pretty great! Get it over at gamereadycourse.com

"Imagination is everything. It is the preview of life's coming attractions."

– Albert Einstein

For those of you who don't think that Pelé or Michael Phelps know what they are talking about, here are some more stories that we found for you.

Olympic diver Troy Dumais, who has competed in four Olympics, says that visualization is important because it can enable athletes to cut off distractions and zero in on the task at hand.

Sports psychologist Karen Cogan also had something to

say about visualization. She emphasized that acrobatic sports like gymnastics and diving can greatly benefit from visualization because it can help these athletes master moves and routines. She said that most athletes in the acrobatic line of sports have to feel whatever routine they want to perform before they can do it. Visualization helps with that.

Fencer Mariel Zagunis used visualization to win two gold medals in the Olympics. She uses the time she's on a flight to go over all the possible scenarios that can arise during the event. She said that she spends time watching her rivals and she knows how they fight. She knows their strengths, their weaknesses, and the surprises that they will try to pull off. She says that in sabre fencing, anything can happen in a split second. She spends her time preparing herself for any situation so that when a situation arises, she is not caught off guard. She has already mentally prepared for it.

Aaron Gordon started using visualization at fourteen years old and Kobe, Tiger, Venus, and Serena Williams used visualization when they were younger as well. It's kind of a thing.

Scientific Studies That Prove Visualization Techniques Work

A study conducted by Richard Suinn, a highly regarded sports psychologist, involved some of the Olympic athletes that he had been working with. Suinn conducted his study with Olympic downhill skiers. He had them ski a run, and during the run, he measured the reaction of the brain and muscles to the skiing activity.

For the second phase of his study, he asked them to imagine skiing in their head. He then studied the brain and muscle activities. He found that during their imagination practice, the brain sent electrical signals that were similar to the signals released in the first physical practice phase of the experiment. He also discovered that the muscle reactions were also similar to when they were skiing.

Another study conducted by Guang Yue, a renowned exercise physiologist, showed how powerful visualization could be to the extent of causing physical changes. In the study, he asked volunteers only to imagine flexing their biceps. After a few weeks of this mental exercise, the participants showed a 13.5% increase in overall strength.

Another study conducted at the University of Chicago required study subjects to visualize shooting free throws in their heads. After one month of doing this, the participants improved their shooting by 23%.

Another study involved three test groups and the practice of shooting free throws. Test group 1 consisted of people who practiced. Test group 2 consisted of people who were told only to visualize their practice, and the last group was told not to practice at all. The first group improved by 24%. The group that didn't practice at all didn't improve, which was expected, and the group that visualized only with no actual practice improved by 23%.

Another study by Aymeric Guillot, Kevin Moschberger, and Christian Collet attempted to see what happens when physical and mental exercises are combined. It showed that when jumpers visualized their jumps and then performed the actual jumps they imagined, they improved their performances by 45%!

Several studies have also confirmed that when a person engages in visualization exercises, a response is triggered by the autonomic nervous system that controls your body and regulates most body functions, such as heart rate and respiratory rate.

Bottom line? USE THIS! USE VISUALIZATION, STARTING NOW! Here's how to do it.

How To Make Visualization Work For You

Visualization is like any other exercise. You have to practice it over and over again. The more you see yourself winning, the more you will win. The more you see yourself performing successfully, the more you will perform successfully. Here's a great exercise that you can do to start exercising your visualization muscles!

Five-Minute Visualization Exercise

Before you play a game, and even before you go to practice, visualize your success either at home or on the car ride to the gym, field, or court. Here are the steps that you should follow to have the most effective visualization practice.

1. Arrive early to the event like Pelé so that you can get your mind familiar with the environment.

2. Find a quiet space before the game, important practice,

or performance.

3. Create the whole event in your mind.

4. See yourself performing successfully. (If you struggle seeing yourself performing successfully, then see yourself with the end result that you want. i.e. holding the trophy, being congratulated by their coach, etc. That's what a jockey did in the audio program the Maverick Mindset by Dr. John Eliot. It worked!)

5. Relax, and replay the whole event over and over again.

Visualization can also help you in the following ways:

- It can help you stay relaxed before or during events.

- It can help you grow and maintain the proper mental state for competing in games.

- It can help you manage your stress and performance anxiety.

- It can help you increase confidence before any competition.

- Whenever you do make a mistake, it can help you handle it well and move past it.

- It can help you appropriately handle losses or bad performances.

Visualization is one of the best things to do to help you become more confident. So, start using it as a part of your get better process. It's like having a practice before practice or playing the game before the game.

Chapter Summary

- Visualization can help you prepare for games effectively.

- Visualization can also reduce your stress and sports anxiety.

- Sports icons use visualization.

- The subconscious mind does not know the difference between what is real and imagined. You can use visualization techniques to feed your subconscious mind with images that can help you bring your vision into reality.

In the next chapter, we are going to talk about writing down your goals. We will also look at the neuroscience behind writing goals down. Then we will look at the qualities of a good goal and good goal writing.

Here is my book suggestion for this chapter. It's a good one!

Chapter 3 Book: *Eleven Rings* By Phil Jackson.

For a complete list of books and resources go to
gamereadycourse.com/

Also... If this book his helping you I'm going to ask you to go and leave a review. Those things mean a lot and they help this book help other people. Just click here https://www.amazon.com/review/create-review/ref=cm_cr_othr_d_wr_but_top?ie=UTF8&channel=glance-detail&asin=B087ZCSB6V or go back to the site where you purchased this book and leave your review. I super appreciate you for doing this!

Chapter 4:
Writing Down Your Goals – Exercise #3

By now I think that you understand that goal setting is good, but are you doing it? Even if you are setting goals, do you know if you are doing it the right way? Basically, if you are not writing down your goals you are not doing it right. If you have been writing down your goals, good job! But if you have not, let me show you why you should start today and the best way to go about it.

Writing down your goals is a way of telling your subconscious mind what you want it to achieve with a direct injection of information. Writing down your goals ties the mental to the physical. Remember, the subconscious mind is actively listening. By writing down your goals you are etching your goals in mental stone.

Let me show you a few examples of how it has worked for a friend of mine.

"I am highly recruited by Pac 12 schools."

– D'Shawn Schwartz

My friend D'Shawn Schwartz wrote that sentence when he was still in seventh grade. Senior year he was highly recruited by Pac 12 schools and, as of the time of writing this book, he plays for the Colorado Buffs Men's Basketball Team (a Pac 12 school).

Do you know that Michael Phelps had a goal to train seven days a week, 365 days a year – and it was also written down? Imagine having a goal to train every single day! Obviously, his goal worked out for him, but he also committed to writing down his goals. Writing down your goals works!

Why Do I Have To Write My Goals Down?

Writing down your goals does three major things for you. The first and most important thing is that it gives you clarity around your goals and dreams. You don't doubt what you want to achieve as much because you are writing it down every day! Writing down your goals and dreams helps you cut off the distractions that will trip up your peers. Have you heard the expression, "If you repeat anything often enough it becomes the truth"? Well, if you write it down it often enough becomes a law that your subconscious mind must obey.

Second, writing down your goals tells your subconscious mind that you mean business because when you write down your goals, you pass it through the logic section of the brain, the section that is 100% literal. The subconscious mind becomes aware that you need that specific goal achieved and it gets to work. It's actually scientifically proven. Here's an article about how it all works.

Forbes **Article: "Neuroscience Explains Why You**

Need To Write Down Your Goals If You Actually Want To Achieve Them." (Excerpt)

Writing things down happens on two levels: external storage and encoding. External storage is easy to explain: you're storing the information contained in your goal in a location (e.g. a piece of paper) that is very easy to access and review at any time. You could post that paper in your office, on your refrigerator, etc. It doesn't take a neuroscientist to know you will remember something much better if you're staring at a visual cue (aka reminder) every single day.

But there's another deeper phenomenon happening: encoding. Encoding is the biological process by which the things we perceive travel to our brain's hippocampus where they're analyzed. From there, decisions are made about what gets stored in our long-term memory and, in turn, what gets discarded. Writing improves that encoding process. In other words, when you write it down it has a much greater chance of being remembered.

Lastly, when you write down your goals, you become more aware of the opportunities available to achieve those goals. Writing down your goals helps your mind focus on achieving your goals because writing them down makes them resonate more loudly in your subconscious mind. Some call it activating your reptilian activating system. That's basically where you are looking for something and suddenly that something that you never noticed before is everywhere. Playing slug bug is a good example of how your reptilian activating system works. Before the game, you don't see VW bugs anywhere. During the game, they are suddenly everywhere!

To add more power to your written goals, share them with your parents or mentor. It is super important that someone who believes in your abilities is aware of your goals. It's also important to have someone hold you accountable. You wrote your goals down didn't you? Good! Then this part should be easy!

If you're asking, "Is there proof that a written goal is more likely to be achieved than a thought or said goal?" Uhh . . . Yeah! You know me. I got the studies to prove it. We out here!

Let's start by looking at a study done by Dr. Gail Matthews, at the Dominican University in California. In the experiment, Dr. Matthews gathered 267 people from different parts of the world and different professions. She split them into two groups—one group of people who wrote down their goals, and the other group of people who didn't.

I think that you can probably guess how it went. The group that regularly wrote down their goals achieved them at a significantly higher rate than those who didn't. She also discovered that those who wrote down their goals and dreams regularly achieved their goals at a significantly higher rate than those who didn't. The group that wrote down their goals was 42% more likely to reach them. That's a lot of percentages! Why wouldn't you want to increase your chances for success? It literally takes five minutes out of your day.

The Wrap-Up!

So basically, your brain has two sides to it—the right and the left hemispheres. The right hemisphere is primarily imaginative. It is responsible for all of your imagination. The left hemisphere is literal. It is responsible for all of your reasoning and critical thinking. They are connected by something called the corpus callosum, which allows for electrical signals from both hemispheres to make contact. These electrical signals communicate with the rest of our body. They basically help us convert our thoughts into reality.

If you only think about your goals, you are only using the right part of your brain. That part is meant for imagination. But if you write them down, you are tapping into the abilities of the left part that is literal and logic based. Writing down your goals brings both parts of your brain together. Writing is not an imaginative practice. You are actually physically writing something down.

When you write down your goals, you give your subconscious mind a new form of ideas, productivity, and consciousness, which means that your subconscious mind becomes able to see possibilities that are hidden from your conscious mind. Here's how to do it best.

Five-Minute Visualization Exercise

Write down your short-term (or daily/weekly) goals before you go to bed and again when you wake up. Those are the times of day when their subconscious mind is most receptive to ideas. Write them down twice daily and watch the magic happen.

You should have daily, weekly, monthly, yearly, and lifetime goals. The daily and weekly goals are the short-term goals and those are the ones that you write down every day. The rest are goals that you can write down once and read or post somewhere in your room to read throughout the day. Work toward your short-term goals daily.

An example of a daily goal could be to shoot the ball five times during a game or shoot the ball 500 times a day. It's good to start with goals that you can control. Making goals at the beginning that you can't control can be frustrating. Notice that I didn't say *make* 500 shots, I said to *take* 500 shots. Once you are a little further down the road you can put some focus on results.

However, if you are practicing and using these tools you will never have to focus on results. Control the controllables and forget the rest. You can control how many shots you take. You can't always control if it goes in or not. You can control how many volleys you hit. You can't always control how they come off of your hand. You can control how many swings you take. You can't always control if you connect with the ball. No matter what the goal is, make sure that you are always pushing yourself.

Bonus: Goal Setting Tips!

Goals Should Be Specific

In the beginning, everyone thinks goals look like this, "I want to play in the NBA." That is a good goal, but it falls short of being specific. A specific goal would be something like this:

"I play in the NBA. I get drafted in the first round. I win 5 NBA championships throughout my career. I retire to run my own software company that increases the profitability of the work from home workforce by 75%."

Discuss your goals with your parents or mentors to make sure that your goals are more specific. For instance, Kobe Bryant had a goal of wanting to play in the NBA for the Los Angeles Lakers. As we all know, he was originally drafted by the Charlotte Hornets and Michael Jordan. However, his subconscious mind knew what the goal was, and the rest is history. See what I mean? Your subconscious mind is amazing!

After going over your goals and breaking them down into smaller, more specific goals, the next stage is strategizing how to achieve those goals. For example, if you want to be the Michael Phelps of your generation, one of your goals should be to learn how to take fewer breaths and master breath control. You see how manageable this goal is, right? Follow this example when setting your goals and remember this is a marathon, not a sprint!

Goals Should Not Be Based On Outcomes

This is a common mistake young athletes make. Don't get me wrong. It's good to want to win every single time. Who doesn't want that? Ronaldo and Ibrahimović are notorious for this, and so are 99.99% of all of the people who we call sports icons. Nobody is cool with losing.

However, your goal, at least in the beginning, should be controllable. Set goals like "I kick 2 shots at the goal or take 5 shots a game or I swing at every fastball or curveball." Those goals are controllable.

Tell yourself that if you do those things then you win. This is how you do it in the beginning. In middle school and at the beginning of high school nobody cares about your wins and losses. You are either getting better or adjusting to a new level of play. Just focus on doing that right now. Focus on getting better. Do not focus on wins and losses. Focus on getting better!

Pro Tip: Until the tenth grade, the best thing to do is to focus on getting better. The best thing to do is to focus on skill work. Do you know Jamal Murray, the point guard for the Denver Nuggets? Well, Jamal Murray's dad didn't even allow him to play consistently on an AAU team until the tenth grade. Until then they worked on skill. As we were told by his family friend and PGC basketball founder Mano Watsa, Jamal would play for a summer. Learn what he had to work on and work on it all the following summer. Then come back and try it out for a summer to see where he was. I think that it worked out for him.

Don't take my word for it. Take a listen to someone who knows the family personally. Just go gamereadycourse.com to hear the interview.

You know who almost didn't even play his junior year because he was going to work on skill only that summer? Michael Porter Junior almost spent the entire summer working on skill as well. He played because he wanted to be ranked, and playing AAU was the best path to that.

All this to say, remember that this is a development time and focusing on skill is the real goal. NOT WINS! What were LeBron James's middle school stats? How about Michael Phelps? How about Megan Rapinoe? How about Simone Biles? Exactly! For now, just get better!

Reward Yourself When You Reach Your Smaller Goals

Celebrate your successes and recognize your failures. You need both. I like to do it this way. If your failure energy is at a 9 when you fail, then your success energy when you succeed should be at a 9,000!

You need the criticism that comes with correction and accountability when you fall short, and you need the big parade when you do well. After the correction or the parade is over, be sure to ask what you can do better. The journey toward getting better is never over.

"It really doesn't bother me because my dad was my first hater, so if I can take it from him, I can take it from anybody." – Ja Morant, Memphis Grizzlies (when asked how he will deal with critics).

Writing Down Your Goals Process Summarized

So, now you are writing down your goals, yes? You have some tips on how to do it. Here's the summary of this chapter.

Write Down Your Goals (In The Present Tense)

After you've gone over the goals and broken them into manageable pieces, write them down in the present tense. For example, "I take five shots in every game." By writing it like this, you are giving your subconscious mind effective commands.

If you say things in future tense your subconscious mind is set to seek but never receive mode. For instance, saying things like, "Next year I will make . . ." or "Next game I will shoot . . . or "Tomorrow I will . . ." tells your subconscious mind to do it next time or tomorrow. Every day your subconscious mind will think *not this game, but next game, or next year, or tomorrow.*

It is never tomorrow. It is always today. Write your goals in the present tense so that your subconscious mind can help you.

Make Your Goals Specific

Make your goals specific. That means make a list of goals on your way to your big goal and also make a list of goals that you want to achieve after you reach your big goal. Motivational speaker Eric Thomas was once in a room with a bunch of NFL players. They were having a struggling season and couldn't figure out why. Mr. Thomas told them that their problem was that most of the players' goals were to make it to the NFL. Now that they had made it, their subconscious minds were in relax mode. They needed new goals.

Don't fall into that trap. Make all of your goals and make

them very specific. For instance, here is how I would suggest for you to write down your goals.

1. I beat my opponent off of the line of scrimmage every time.

2. I have 5 tackles every game.

3. I am highly recruited by SEC schools.

4. I am drafted in the first round.

5. I help my team win 4 Super Bowls.

6. I retire with the St. Louis Rams.

7. I start a tech company that helps people work from home.

8. I visit 25 countries with my family.

You get the idea. Make goals for every step of your journey. When you make it to your next goal, you want to have another goal waiting for your subconscious mind to work on.

Write Your Goals Down Every Day

This is one of the easiest and most difficult things to do. It takes a touch of discipline. Writing down your goals every day tells your subconscious mind that we have something to do today. It also supercharges your goal-setting mechanism. Write them down! EVERY DAY!

Celebrate Your Wins And Hold Yourself Accountable For Your Losses

Acknowledge your failures and celebrate your successes. Also, be open to criticism. It's a part of the process.

Remember what Michael Jordan's mom said to him when he got cut from his high school basketball team. She didn't say, "You're better than all of those kids. Your coach is crazy." She didn't say, "Let's go get some ice cream. Let's not talk about basketball right now." She didn't say, "I'm sorry honey. I can see that you are disappointed right now. Tell me how this makes you feel." She said . . .

"Michael, you need to discipline yourself."– Deloris Jordan

She knew that he hadn't been working hard enough. She knew that he wasn't the best player on the team at that time. Even Michael said that in high school his brother Larry was the better basketball player. She also knew that he could be great. She knew that he had to discipline himself to get there. Criticism is great!

In the next chapter, we gone talk about YouTube, Instagram, and TikTok! I'm going to introduce you to something called the engraving technique. I'm going to show you how to use it to help master new skills and boost your in-game confidence.

This chapter's resource recommendation is an audio program on goal setting: It's called "Goals" by Zig Ziglar.

<u>For a complete list of books and resources go to</u>

gamereadycourse.com/

Chapter 5:
Watch The Pros! Not The Joes –
Exercise #4

D id you know that you can increase your in-game skills just by watching your idols perform those same skills in your chosen sport? It's called the engraving technique.

The Engraving Technique

In his book *The Little Book of Talent*, Daniel Coyle talks about something that he called the engraving technique. The technique shows that young athletes can improve their talents if they continually and consistently watch top performers in their field perform the skills that they wish to get better at doing. Daniel Coyle proved that when young athletes watch these top performers over and over again, they engrave the skills in their subconscious mind and develop an HD mental blueprint for those skills.

When it comes to learning a skill, reading an instructive book on it is good, listening to a trainer talk about it is also good, but the engraving technique is even better. Several top athletes have used it to become the stars we know them as today.

Here is some proof of how the engraving technique works.

Timothy Gallwey, a great tennis teacher and author, demonstrated the engraving technique in a video that was aired on an old TV show *60 Minutes* back in the day. He had a group of middle-aged people who were new to the game of tennis participate in this experiment. At the beginning of the experiment, he studied their abilities through a couple of tests. He then picked one student who showed the least amount of skill in the group. He made the student focus on him and watch his actions while he performed tennis skills. After twenty minutes of this exercise, the student who was the worst at the skill showed a lot of improvement. When that same student started physically practicing their improvement shot through the roof!

Surprising, isn't it?

Another example is the Suzuki method for learning music that was developed by Shinichi Suzuki, a Japanese violinist. The method emphasizes the need to provide students with a musical environment that is kind of like the linguistic environment we use for learning a language.

Suzuki believed that this type of learning could be replicated in a music learning environment, and that is exactly what he did. Every day, students learning through the Suzuki method listen to several professional recordings of songs that were graded from simple (like "Twinkle, Twinkle, Little Star") to more complex tunes. The songs were performed by masters of the violin so that the students got to hear high-level musicians play the songs that they were working on. As the students listened to these songs, just like a toddler listens to language, the songs become engraved in their minds. Pretty cool huh?

How To Use The Engraving Technique

Think about how Kobe Bryant used the engraving technique to become a player on the level of his mentor and idol Michael Jordan. He watched Michael and studied him so much that Gatorade made commercials where they were changed out with each player because their in-game moves were pretty much identical.

Today, professional athletes are using the engraving technique to achieve high-level goals. It is such a phenomenon that *The Wall Street Journal* wrote about the use of YouTube and how these athletes are crediting improvements to watching videos. In the article, Jayson Tatum talks about how he would watch YouTube and work on the moves that he saw his favorite players do. He would watch, pause the video, practice it, and rewind it to watch it again.

Just take a look at what it did for him. Yeah! If you have the free download that comes with the book you can see him yelling at LeBron James after he scored on him.

Can you see how far this technique can take you? You won't stop at the stage of getting autographs from your idols, you will compete with them professionally. You can read the full *Wall Street Journal* article over at gamereadycourse.com/ and see the pic of Jayson going at LeBron. He #different! You can be too! Take a look over on the download!

How To Use The Engraving Technique Effectively

Just like most other techniques, there is a correct and incorrect way to practice the engraving technique. Let me show you how you perform this technique effectively.

Make a playlist of things that you want to master. Like a Steph Curry 3-point shooting playlist or a Kyrie Irving finishing around the rim playlist. You should not just watch random videos of random players; you should watch videos of the skill you want to master. You should watch high level players performing those skills. While you are watching you should imagine what it feels like to do the skill.

Watching your favorite stars participate and dominate in actual high-level competitions will put you in a competitive state of mind.

If you want to excel in your chosen sports, watch the pros.

Five-Minute Engraving Technique Exercise

We all know who people tell us that we play like. We also know what we need to work on. Like when Richard Williams wrote, "Serena, you need to learn to put more topspin on the ball." Here's what you should do. Find videos on YouTube of a current professional athlete who is great at performing that one skill that you need to work on. Dedicate at least fifteen minutes of your time EVERY DAY to engrave a skill that is relevant to your chosen sport.

Chapter Summary

- Athletes can improve their performance if they watch the pros perform.

- Watching the pros is inspirational, educational, and increases confidence.

- Young athletes can use the engraving technique to learn from their role models.

In the next chapter, you will learn about the meditation technique that athletes like Kobe use. I am going to show you how meditation can be used to eliminate sports anxiety, boost game confidence, and increase overall mental toughness.

For a complete list of books and resources go to gamereadycourse.com/

Chapter 6:
The Meditation Workout – Exercise #5

Meditate to keep it straight

Meditation is one of the mental toughness keys that a lot of us don't pay ANY attention to. Did you know that Michael Jordan, LeBron James, Shaquille O'Neal, Aaron Gordon, Zach Levine, *and* Kobe Bryant all meditated to achieve focus? Why would you not meditate?

That's kind of like hearing that Simone Biles watches Corey Kenshin before gymnastic meets and not at least trying to watch him a couple of times before your game. For those of you who don't know, let me explain to you exactly what meditation is.

According to the Cambridge online dictionary, meditation is: the act of giving your attention to only one thing, either as a religious activity or as a way of becoming calm and relaxed.

Now I am not talking about the religious practice part. I am talking about the clearing your mind and learning how to focus part. Meditation is as simple as clearing your mind. However, like most things, everyone tends to overthink it. Make sure that you keep meditation simple. Meditation is how elite athletes learn how to get into something called flow. Flow is basically where you are playing or performing pretty much on autopilot.

If you've been in sports for a while, chances are that you have heard of "flow state" or the "zone." Lots of elite athletes talk about it, and there's even buzz around it in the media. Do you ever wonder how they get into the zone?

Being in the zone or experiencing flow is like being in that moment when Michael Jordan can't miss because shooting a ball feels like throwing pebbles in the ocean. It's that feeling when Missy Franklin feels like the water is almost pushing her toward the finish line. It's that Odell Beckham Jr. one hand catch for a touchdown moment. Flow is active meditation.

When you are in the zone, it seems like you have lost touch with the real world because you are now in your own world, a world without distractions. In flow the only thing that matters is what you are doing right then. It's kind of like when your mom comes storming into your room because she has been calling you for the last ten minutes, but you were focused on that YouTube video that we talked about watching earlier or your favorite video game. You couldn't hear her because you were in the zone. You were focused 100% on that YouTube video. Experiencing flow and being in the zone is the same thing. You can use that if you want. You're welcome.

Seriously though, flow is like that last time you were playing a video game you liked and you lost track of time, and when you looked up it was a few hours later. That feeling of time flying by and you can't remember what happened to the time!

That's the experience of the zone. Different people can enter the zone in different ways. But one thing we know is that it often occurs when you are doing something you love. We also know that the days you enter the zone and lose track of time are usually your most productive days.

Athletes who operate from the zone are more effective in their games. And coincidentally enough, this status is achieved more often by people who meditate.

The thirteen-time PGA tour winner, Mark Calcavecchia, has described what it feels like when he gets in the zone in a game. We all know how technical the game of golf can be. Players have to consider several factors, such as distance, wind, the shots, and even people at the gallery. But Mark said that whenever he gets into the zone, he doesn't think about any of these factors. All he does is just pull his club and swing away.

Has it been working for him? I'll let his thirteen PGA titles answer that question for you. He is not the only athlete who has testified to the wonders of getting into the zone. Kobe talked about the zone all of the time.

The zone cuts off distractions and allows you to focus on what truly matters. This is why athletes who achieve flow are more calm and peaceful in their games. It's why Chris Rock can yell at Kobe Bryant from ten feet away and Kobe not hear him. I put the photo of Kobe being in the zone and Chris

Rock trying to get him out of the zone. You can see the photo over on the free download or you can just google it.

Scientific Proof Of The Nature Of "The Zone"

Since 1992, several studies have been conducted on the zone. All of them agree that the zone is related to an optimal performance experience in sports. Researchers have looked for ways to induce flow in athletes, and they all seem to agree that it can be done with mindfulness meditation.

Another study, the "Effects of a Mindfulness Intervention on Sports-Anxiety, Pessimism, and Flow in Competitive Cyclists" by J Scott-Hamilton, showed that athletes who are in a flow state showed the highest optimal state while those in regular states had the least optimal state. Basically, athletes in flow performed better and were more relaxed than those who weren't in flow.

Aside from getting control of sports anxiety and boosting performance, meditation also has a lot of other benefits. Meditation has been known to . . .

- Reduce pain: Studies have shown that meditation can reduce sensitivity to pain. Google "Kobe shoots free throws with a torn Achilles" for an example of that.

- Reduce stress: Meditation can be used to manage and reduce stress.

- Increase in-game productivity and ability.

Keep The Small Things Small – (Me), Troy Horne

Remember that just like everything that you do, practicing meditation is going to require time. Could you imagine walking down the street and thinking left foot, right foot, left foot, right foot, left foot, right foot, breathe in, breathe out, blink, repeat? Yeah. . . . You would go crazy. That would be exhausting, yet that is what most young players are doing when they are struggling with mental toughness. They are thinking things like:

- I missed

- The coach doesn't like me

- My teammates don't like me

- I don't like me

- My parents are angry

- My parents are happy

And so on. That's a lot! Meditation helps you clear your mind and perform to the best of your ability. Research shows that anxiety and a feeling of pressure without mindfulness can be some of the greatest enemies of the zone. Meditation will help you get rid of those feelings of pressure and anxiety.

Sports anxiety and flow state cannot coexist—one must go for the other to stay. And I think I know the one you would want to go away.

Let me show you another reason why you should start meditating. Sports anxiety does not only come in the form of fear of performance; for some athletes, it is also fear of being injured in a game. A study discovered that athletes who nursed this type of anxiety were five times more likely to be injured.

That being said, start meditating now! It's super important.

In the previous chapter, we discussed visualization and how it can help achieve goals by engraving it first. I'm going to encourage you to visualize immediately after meditating. If there is a skill that you've been trying to perfect, then you can more easily visualize yourself performing it after meditating.

Finally, don't expect to be perfect at meditating on the first try. Meditation is a practice. Just try it for the next 10 days and see how much better you feel. The more you practice, the easier it will be. Each day, practice the exercise for at least 5 minutes because that is the time it takes the brain to achieve an alpha state of relaxation.

Five-minute meditation exercise. Meditate one time a day for five minutes. It's best to do it in the morning, as Kobe says, but you can do it any time during the day. The point is that you do it.

Here's what you do.

1. Find a quiet space.

2. Imagine yourself sitting on the banks of a calmly flowing river.

3. As you sit there, quiet your mind.

4. Any and every thought that comes into your mind, and there will be many at first, attach to a log and let it float down the river.

5. The goal is not to have an empty river, but to have fewer logs floating down the river than you did when you started. No logs are mastery level stuff!

6. Set a timer so there is one less thought that you have to attach to a log.

7. Do this daily for the next 10 days and if you want, keep going!

Get ready for Mamba-like focus and mental toughness.

The book that I am going to suggest for this chapter is *The Mindful Athlete* By George Mumford. Mr. Mumford was a meditation coach for Michael Jordan, Kobe Bryant, and lots of other pro athletes.

<u>For a complete list of books and resources go to</u>
<u>gamereadycourse.com/</u>

Chapter Summary

- You can use meditation to achieve clarity of mind.

- You can visualize immediately after meditating.

- The zone is a state where you have a sense of control, clear goals, and a lack of self-awareness.

- You can use meditation to achieve the zone.

In the next chapter, we are going to go over the power of

playing small and how it has changed the world of youth sports. See you in the next chapter.

Chapter 7:
Learn To Play Small – Exercise #6

Make Everything Smaller

Have you ever heard the story about the game Futsal? Well, it is quite an interesting one. Everyone knows that South American soccer is some of the greatest soccer in the world. Needless to say, they tend to dominate in the world cup matches and consistently make appearances in the finals. They do so well that larger countries started to ask, "How do these poorer countries with a quarter of the resources train at a high enough level to even compete with the larger countries and their enormous football/soccer budgets?" The answer they found was a game called Futsal.

In Futsal, everything is smaller. The ball is smaller. The court is smaller and harder, and the goals are also smaller. That means that pretty much everything is more difficult to do. Imagine going from that to a bigger ball, a softer pitch, and a larger goal. As you can imagine, after playing a season or two of Futsal, soccer feels like shooting fish in the proverbial barrel.

The kids in Brazil are accustomed to playing in dusty,

rocky streets. These streets cause the ball to react unpredictably because it could hit a rock and bounce off in the wrong direction. These kids still manage to get the ball going, and even dare to show off high level skills. What do you think is happening to their abilities when they play on smaller, more challenging courts? What do you think will happen when they finally get the opportunity to play in a decent pitch with level ground? Answer: they will perform better because they've done the hard work in the streets and improved their skill in a more difficult situation.

It is not only in Brazil that you find intentional constraints in football. In Spain, there are stories of how youth coaches create small-sided games that can help their players develop quick transitions when playing the game. It's no wonder that the Spanish football team is known for that quick transition play that is now called "tiki-taka."

Some individual players are direct results of constraint training. One example is Neymar. Even if you are not a football lover, I am sure that you've heard of that name before. Neymar is the product of Futsal, and some analysts argue that it is Futsal that made him a superstar. If you've ever watched the man play, you know that his style of play is different from what is generally acceptable in conventional football. Stories have it that he started playing Futsal at an early age, and he would use the skills he picked up on the streets to tease opponents when he later joined The Santos football club.

What about Ronaldinho? This superstar actively plays beach soccer, which is, of course, notorious for its sandy, hard to play on pitch. For a footballer, you would think he would only play in level pitches, but he knows what you now know.

Another superstar, Mesut Özil, improves his game by playing cage soccer. Have you ever seen players playing conventional football in a cage? So, what is this young player doing kicking football in a cage? You won't ask questions like these when you realize that Mesut Ozil is the assist king of the English Premier League.

Petr Čech, the man that excellently kept Chelsea's posts for several years and later went on to Arsenal to repeat the same feat, also has his way of imposing constraints in his practice. He catches ping pong balls from a machine. Who does that, considering how small ping pongs are when compared to a soccer ball.

It is always good to step out of your comfort zone and try something different. This is the argument against just practicing on normal size courts or fields all of the time. Football in England is played strictly by rules. Even when young players try to be creative with the ball, they are quickly reminded that they need to stay within the confines of the rules. With this type of training, what you will get are players who cannot adapt to changes.

These experiences and factors can shape a young athlete's future for the better. Play smaller, but always, ALWAYS play free!

The Science

Here is some theoretical evidence that supports playing small.

Karl Newell defined three primary categories of constraints: task, person, and environment. He says that these categories interact to shape motor control and coordination, especially in young athletes. Karl's approach to development is known as the Constraints-Led Approach to skill acquisition.

What is a constraint? Constraints are factors that create limitations so that some possibilities and actions are excluded, while other possibilities and actions are left for the athlete to explore. One thing we know for sure is that the absence of constraints breeds a lack of creativity.

When you introduce constraints, you get an athlete who is creative and resourceful because they are accustomed to finding success even when limitations are imposed on them. This reminds me of the old saying, "Necessity is the mother of invention." When the constraints come hard, your talent will have no choice but to adapt.

What this concept of constraint training does is help athletes transfer their talents into environments that are free of constraints, allowing them to outperform athletes that don't train with constraints. We see that the interaction of constraints can guide and shape skills and behaviors.

To use Karl's approach, you will need to manipulate both the environmental and individual constraints to facilitate deep engagement in your training sessions.

While it may be difficult for you to look for ways to tweak the practice activities to create these constraints, realize that this is the common challenge. In 2015, a study found that when looking at the development of European players, Spanish coaches commit more time to plan tasks that develop the skills their players need. Don't worry though. As Michelle Obama said: "I've been at every powerful table you can think of. They are not that smart." All of that to say, if they can do it you can do it!

The Application Process

Practicing small is a confidence builder, and we use it all the time. Now, I feel like I should warn you that most people will think that doing stuff like this is ridiculous, but imagine what they were saying to Richard Williams. You are in great company. Find a way to make your practices more difficult by making the court smaller, making the ball smaller, or making the goal smaller. When you move up to the larger court, ball, or goal, you will feel like everything is super easy. Confidence builder—check!

Not every constraint is suitable for every personality or sport. Let me give you a guide on choosing the constraints to incorporate in you or your kid's practice.

- Always identify the skill you want to develop.

- Develop a constraint that is hinged on that skill.

- Play the game smaller.

Five-minute practice small exercise. Ok, this one is

going to take more than five minutes. Sorry about that, but we stuck to the five minutes thing this far. Real talk: sometimes greatness takes more than five minutes. Greatness isn't easy.

Find a way to make your practice more difficult by making the objects in your game smaller. If you're a golfer, practice with a smaller club head. If you are a football player, practice with a smaller ball. If you are a baseball player, practice with a smaller bat. Find a way to make the objects in the game smaller during practice and watch your skill level shoot through the roof.

The book for this chapter is *The Talent Code* by Daniel Coyle.

For a complete list of books and resources go to

gamereadycourse.com

Chapter Summary

- Calculated constraints can make you more creative and resilient.

- Take yourself out of your comfort zones from time to time.

- Make your practice more difficult since fire brings out the best in gold.

In the next chapter, you will learn the importance of practicing slowly. I will show you the advantages of doing this, and then I will also show you the right way to practice and learn a skill.

Chapter 8:
Practice Slower – Exercise #7

Practice Slow

Did you know that Venus and Serena practiced slower? Slowing down your practices every once in a while is a great way to understand all of your movements on a bigger level. Slowing everything down allows you to see and correct every little part of your game. I get it. Thanks to Instagram we want to do the double-cross, between the legs, behind the back jump shots that they put up on Snap, but what some of the younger athletes fail to realize is that there are levels to doing that shot. You must first understand that you are seeing the finished product and not the building blocks that made that move possible.

Slowing down your practice will allow you to see any of your flaws and correct them. It will allow you to understand and feel when you are not balanced or when your tennis stroke, golf stroke, or bat swing are not right. Slowing down is one of the major keys to mastery.

Sometimes the most effective way to shoot accurately and faster is to take one step back, slow down, and change your approach. Many times, we want to go straight to the results. A lot of the time we aren't interested in all of the little steps that it takes to get there.

Let me just say this. You can't continue with the routines you are used to and expect to get a different result. According to Albert Einstein, that is the definition of insanity.

The results that you get without breaking things down and practicing slowly like the pros will not be great. It's not that you can't do that amazing move that you saw on Instagram, it's just that you haven't worked on the mastery part that the pro worked on off-camera. If you start with mediocre techniques and then add speed to those mediocre techniques, you are going to end up with a mediocre result.

There Is A Better Way

The key is slowing down and looking at your performances and practice. The truth is that a lot of your problems are very noticeable when you slow everything down, but since you are not slowing down, your mistakes go unnoticed. The top performers in every field understand the need for slowing down and taking stock of everything they're doing. Once you learn this technique, you should use it.

"Slow training" is one of the most effective training techniques out there. Ironic as it may sound, slow training is important for developing speed. Don't make the mistake of thinking that slow training will make you a slower athlete. It will help you develop high-quality speed.

Shot putters, javelin, or hammer athletes can achieve their throws in a ridiculously short time. They can perform complex motor skills at a rate that is impossible for others. When you watch them perform, you will notice that the time they take to execute these skills is too short for them to have thought about the individual movements.

The same thing goes for pianists, drummers, and just about any other professional who has slowly honed their skills. Did these professionals start their profession playing fast? No! They took baby steps. They developed their skills slowly and took their time to perfect it.

The slow training method means that you repeat each of your skills slowly, the same way, every time until it comes to you automatically. Also, never attempt to combine mastering two skills at once. Give each skill enough time to register in your subconscious by itself. When you are certain that the first skill was ingrained in your mind, then move on to the next. Professional athletes never move on until they are sure they have perfected the first skill.

After this, speed will happen naturally. That's how it works. You will not be slow because you started slow. You will actually be faster on the court, field, or pitch because you took your time to put the essentials of the game together. Slowly.

Why Slow Down?

Many people don't know this, but there was a whole summer when Steph Curry didn't shoot outside the paint. An ENTIRE SUMMER! He had to slow down and learn to rework his shot in order to get better. Doing this allowed him to become one of the greatest shooters in NBA history. Slowing down amplifies all your mistakes and inefficiencies and allows you to correct them.

This deliberate muscle memory work ingrains the correct movement into your mind and allows you to not only do the 10,000 hours that Malcolm Gladwell talks about, but to roll in the deliberate practice element that Anders Ericsson talks about as well.

Practice doesn't make perfect. Perfect practice makes perfect.

– Vince Lombardi

The Science

Do you know that the faster a stimulus is, the harder it is for your brain to pick out details? For instance, if you were standing at the subway and a train comes and just zooms past you, the only thing you might remember about this train is the color. But if this same train had approached you slowly, the chances are that you would be able to pick out the shape of the front lights, the style of the doors, and you might even pick out the clothing on some of the passengers.

This principle is known as the Weber-Fechner law:

"As stimulus increases, the brain's ability to pick out details drops."

Another explanation is that when you repeatedly, slowly practice a skill, a neural pathway is created in the brain. It's kind of like a tunnel for your memory to travel down every time you need it. But if this neural pathway is not protected by something called myelin, the tunnel for your memory can be blocked or changed by performance-reducing agents like adrenaline and cortisol.

How can you protect this pathway? You guessed it, by slow and consistent practice. Neuroscience shows that if you slowly and consistently practice a skill, the insulating sheath of myelin will surround the formed neural pathway and protect it from getting wrecked by stress or anxiety. What this means is that you can perform that particular skill no matter how stressed you are. Give yourself a better chance at becoming elite and practice slow once in a while.

Five minutes slow down exercise – Before every part of your practice, walk through the drill that you are about to do in slow motion. This will allow you to see what you're doing wrong and fix it. Slow down every drill for one or two reps before you do it at full speed.

Chapter Summary

- If you flood your brain with signals, the brain will not be able to pick up subtle details that can be used to improve your game.

- The key to learning a skill is taking it slowly and doing it repeatedly until it becomes part of the subconscious mind.

- When you learn a skill at a subconscious level, you can do it very quickly, even in very stressful conditions, like the ones in competitive games.

In the next chapter, we will look at some reasons why you must ensure that you don't always train in a nice facility. I will also show you how you can train roughly for more mental toughness.

Chapter 9:
Train Rough – Exercise #8

Muhammad Ali Inspired Rocky To Train Rough

I get it! Most of us want to work out in a state-of-the-art facility, with nice locker rooms and brand-new gym floors or courts. However, this is one of the worst things that you can do when you are trying to get better. Those types of gyms are a signal to your subconscious mind to rest. Training in nice gyms is a signal to the mind that you have arrived, that you have already succeeded and reached your goal. Training rough is a signal to the subconscious mind to get to work; the goal is still out of reach.

This is why the Russian gymnasts dominated the Olympics for decades. Their training facility was not the best. This is why bodybuilders like Ronnie Coleman tend to train in gyms with rusty weights and old weight machines. This is why all of the talent hotbeds in Daniel Coyle's *The Talent Code* were dinky little facilities with old equipment and broken-down stuff all over the place. This is why Jerry Rice played on dirt football fields with very little grass at Mississippi Valley State. This is why Michael Phelps worked out at the North Baltimore Aquatic Club. This club was nothing different than an old YMCA with rusty pool fixtures and old windows. It has been updated since Michael trained there, but back in the day it was as regular as regular gets.

This is why Muhammad Ali went to the woods in Pennsylvania to train after losing to a young Leon Spinks. Training rough helped him become a three-time heavyweight champion and one of the greatest heavyweight boxers of all time. Muhammad's training inspired Sylvester Stallone to write the same type of training experience in his movie *Rocky* when Rocky was going to train to fight in *Rocky IV*. Training rough is one of the few physical parts of training your mind.

Is There A Logical Explanation For This?

Of course there is. Uncertainty and struggle are signals for the brain to start learning and to start working. Do you ever wonder how hip-hop artists go from being poor to making hundreds of millions of dollars like Jay-Z? Try living in Marcy Projects for five minutes and then being given an opportunity to change your life and get out. You'll get it. Do you ever wonder how Richard Williams could raise two of the greatest tennis players to ever play the game? Try living in Compton California back in the late 80s early 90s.

This uncertainty is your subconscious mind's motivational speaker. Start practicing in a less flashy environment and see how your mental toughness will grow. See how your skill level will grow.

A Yale study tried to identify the changes the brain undergoes when it is faced with uncertainties. In the study, they presented monkeys with tasks that have different outcomes. Then they checked the differences that their brains underwent with the two tasks.

When the monkeys were presented with the tasks that had a fixed outcome, the scientist noticed reduced activity in the frontal cortex. This was attributed to the fact that these animals knew the outcome of the task. When the outcomes were uncertain, the scientist detected more brain activity.

Stability Tells The Subconscious Mind To Take A Break

When you are practicing on a familiar pitch, field, or basketball court with familiar faces all of the time, your mind is relaxed and stable. The brain senses this stability and goes to sleep because it has nothing to worry about. However, if you go to a rougher facility, a poorly kept football field, or a roughly kept volleyball or baseball field, for instance, uncertainty has been introduced. This makes the brain more alert and more agile. So, if you want to maximize your learning, you must train rough.

Those situations that you may consider uncomfortable are the situations that will increase your brain activity and help you learn faster. This alertness is what you want to tap into. That is why I am suggesting that you train away from your comfort zone, just like Mohammed Ali, Venus and Serena Williams, and Jay-Z did.

How Do You Train Rough?

Now don't go all crazy and cancel your memberships to your cushy gyms if you don't want to. However, I would suggest finding a hole in the wall facility to go to every once in a while. Remember, Muhammad used this as a tool—not a constant, but as an added place to work out.

You still want to have access to a nice workout facility and high-level training. However, I would suggest you add an element of roughness to your routine. It's key to taking your game to the next level. Find your rough training situation and visit it often.

Other Practical Ways You Step Out Of Your Comfort Zone

I know that you can't always go to the woods like Mohammed Ali. Your parents may not be willing or able to take you. But there are more subtle ways that you can bring rough training into your training routine.

Wake up early to train. It is never appealing to leave a nice warm bed, but if you can get up and do a few practices in the early morning, you can learn faster. This is also a great way to build the mental toughness that you need to excel in sports. If you've ever been to a military camp, you know that they never miss their early morning drills. Start copying the military. Also, make sure that the exercise or mental toughness technique you are using is suitable for your age. Realize that you are still growing and that you need rest to grow physically. You have time.

Try something new. I know you have routines for developing every aspect of your game, but how many times have you tried to throw in something new? This is a good way to throw in some uncertainty. You can research new, different ways to achieve the desired skills and try them out. The uncertainty that comes from the new method will increase brain activity and you will learn faster.

Your final five-minute training rough exercise – This one is also a little more than five minutes, but it's pretty simple to do. Find a facility that is a little "under the radar" so to speak and hold some of your training sessions there. We're talking about leaving some of the cushy comforts of your regular gym behind. Perhaps there is no A/C, maybe some drafty windows, boards missing in the floor, rusty, dusty weights. You know the drill: train rough and get ready to become a dawg on the floor!

Chapter Summary

- Uncertainty is good for learning. Get out of your comfort zone if you want to learn a new skill faster.

- Stability stops the brain from learning. While in training, ensure that you don't come to the point of excess comfort and stability. That will end the learning process.

In the next and final chapter, we will summarize everything we've learned in this book. I added this chapter because I want to give you a section you can always turn to whenever you are in doubt about what we've covered in this book.

Chapter 10:
The Cooldown

Well, congratulations! You did it! You made it to the end of the book! Time to use what you have learned to become even more mentally tough than you already are. Most kids didn't make it this far. So just by making it to the end, you proved that you are pretty tough and committed. However, going forward, you will face lots of challenges. Sports performance anxiety and low confidence are a part of the process, but it's a controllable part of your sports journey.

These challenges can hamper your performance and may cause you to not live up to your full potential if you let them. When these challenges attack you, don't forget everything you've practiced. Instead, use it like Cus D'amato talked about in the video on the free download. Still need the free download? Go to gamereadycourse.com

The eight exercises that you learned in this book are the keys to controlling these stress and anxiety sports difficulties.

At the beginning of this book, we talked about how the starting point for mental toughness is a mindset. This mindset involves your mentor or your family first. We also talked about how you must decide what you want, and you must not doubt that you can and will achieve it.

We saw Richard Williams who dared to believe that Venus and Serena would grow up to be the greatest female tennis stars before they were even born. We also talked about how he got them to believe in him and in themselves.

We looked at the subconscious mind. Our subconscious minds are powerful tools that control most of our daily activities such as blinking, walking, breathing, etc. If your subconscious mind can help you breathe without you thinking about it, imagine what you will be able to do when you strengthen your subconscious mind with positive thoughts.

We talked about not allowing the fears and failures of others to pollute your subconscious mind. You have to feed your subconscious mind with the things that you want to see. This is very important because your subconscious mind is a judge-free zone. It is not able to tell good thoughts from bad ones. It just works with whatever you feed it. We saw how Richard Williams used the power of the subconscious mind to bring out the best in Venus and Serena. We talked about how he would write in big text what he wanted his girls to work on and paste it right where they would see it.

Post your goals in your room, right where you can see them. Read and write them down every day!

We also looked at visualization techniques, which is another important technique for mental toughness. Visualization is the practice of picturing events in our minds before they happen. Visualization helps you to mentally prepare for the task at hand. It also helps you to prepare responses for anything that might come up during the game.

We saw how the great Pelé and countless other athletes used and are still using visualization to improve their in-game performance. It is also important to realize that visualization is just like any other exercise and needs to be done over and over again in order to be mastered. It is not something you can try once and quit if you fail to see instant results. Mental toughness isn't a social media 60-second results kind of thing—it's something that you need to do for your entire sports life! If you want to be great, that is.

Then we covered writing down your goals. You must write down your goals because doing so gives clarity to your goal and strengthens your subconscious mind to go all out and achieve what you wrote. Writing down your goals tells your mind what it should pay attention to. We saw how athletes like D'Shawn Schwartz used this technique to be pursued by the colleges he wanted and accomplish lots of other things.

When writing down your goals, there are little tweaks that you can do to make this exercise more powerful. For example, write down goals using positive action steps and present tense. These are mental toughness super boosters. We talked about how you bring in both sides of your brain when you write down your goals, and how you only use one side when you just say your goals out loud. We talked about writing down your goals in the morning and at night because that is when your subconscious mind is more receptive to ideas.

Your goals must be specific (not just general). Your goals

must be measurable. Your goals must be unreasonable, and your daily goals must be bite-sized. We also stressed the need for rewards whenever you achieve milestones, because that can serve as an effective morale booster. Celebrating your small wins also builds mental toughness. Seeing yourself achieving your goals and winning is huge!

We talked about the importance of watching the pros in whatever sports you are involved in. NOT THE YOUTH KID WHO MAKES A LOT OF IG VIDEOS. WATCH THE PROS! We saw the engraving technique that Daniel Coyle talked about in his book. This technique helps you look at skills that professionals are performing and imprint them in your mind. This technique tells you that if you focus closely on the skill that is being performed, you can get a high-definition image of it in your subconscious mind. We backed it up with examples like Timothy Gallwey's study on learning tennis and the Suzuki method of learning music. They both showed the power of the engraving technique.

Next, we talked about the meditation technique and how you can use it to clear your mind from distractions and focus on what truly matters, which is the game or task at hand. We saw how meditation will help you achieve the zone, which is a state where nothing else but the game matters.

We talked about the power of playing small. We looked at Futsal as a good example of how playing small can bring out the best in you and your game. Doing this is really going to turn you into a mental toughness monster. I use this for basketball, and it makes the game feel so easy.

We also talked about the technique of practicing slowly.

When you practice slowly, your brain will be able to capture any issues in your practice better. You will know the areas that need fixing. We also learned about focusing on one skill until you master it and then moving on to the next step. When you do this, speed comes naturally. It is better to focus on learning the skill very well before you go into the combo moves.

And finally, we wrapped up our discussion with the need to train rough. We saw how Muhammad Ali chose to practice in the woods rather than a cushy training ring. The brain learns more when it is confronted by uncertainties; uncertainties that we characterized as rough. We saw how science was able to explain this as well. Training rough is the final key to mental toughness and it's kind of awesome! Now it's your turn to take action. Now it's your job to make it real.

Final Words

Being mentally tough as a person is important. As an athlete, you need to be mentally strong and resilient to compete at your peak performance and achieve your maximum athletic potential. Mental toughness isn't what you have, it is what you do, it's what you create. Mental toughness is a skill that can be developed and learned. When you develop your mental toughness, know that it doesn't happen overnight, it is a process that will develop over time, and it is worth every second that you put in because you will see positive results.

It's one thing to learn about this, and it is another thing to put it to practice. Now I am going to be a coach for you right now. If you just read this book and add it to your book collection without putting what you've learned into practice, then you have failed yourself. Practice the techniques we've discussed. They truly are the difference makers that you need to help yourself be a mental toughness beast!

I made it easy for you. You now have eight five-minute mental toughness exercises for each of the techniques we've discussed. All you have to do is put what you've learned into practice. As you get better at these exercises, I want to encourage you to lengthen your practice time. Now that you have the tools of the greats, use them for your mental toughness. You have everything you need to be a Mamba.

Now the question is . . . will you use it? It's now up to you!

See you in the gym. – Moses

Thank you for taking this journey with me. Be sure to get all of the free resources that go along with this book over at gamereadycourse.com. You are going to want to have everything that's over there. I put it together especially for you and it's free!

One Last Thing

If you could leave an honest review for this book on Amazon or on Audible or both I would really appreciate it. Your support really does make a difference and I read all the reviews personally so I can get your feedback and make this book even better.

Thank you for being an awesome athlete and, on behalf of all of the other youth sports athletes out there, thank you for making our youth sports community better.

If you'd like to leave a review then all you need to do is click the review link on this book's page on Amazon here: https://www.amazon.com/review/create-review/ref=cm_cr_othr_d_wr_but_top?ie=UTF8&channel=glance-detail&asin=B087ZCSB6V

Thanks again for your support!

Are You Ready For The Next Level?

FIRST: You need to make sure to listen to our free podcast episodes for athletes at http://hoopchalk.com/. Those episodes were super fun to record. Plus, they have a lot of information in them. You're gonna love them.

SECOND: Make sure that you pick up the "Parent's Guide" of this book if you. It covers how to support your young athlete if you are a parent or a coach.

Mental Toughness For Young Athletes Parent's Guide

Just click the link to get your copy on Amazon:

Mental Toughness For Young Athletes – Parent's Version

Continue Your Mental Toughness Journey With Book 2!

THIRD: Get book #2! This book is filled with next level mental toughness stuff once you get the basics down. You gotta have the foundation before you can go to the advanced stuff. When you're ready, consider this next book as your second degree blackbelt. Click below and get ready to take your mental toughness to the next level!

Just click the link to get your copy on Amazon:

Mental Toughness For Young Athletes Volume 2: GRIT

Other Books By Moses And Troy Horne

Just click the link to get your copy on Amazon:

The AAU Basketball Bible: Everything You'd Better Know About Youth Basketball And College Recruiting

About The Authors

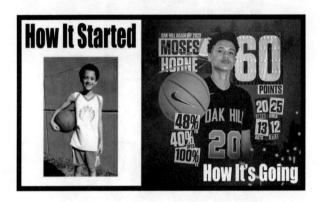

Moses Horne is a high school basketball player who started playing basketball in the fifth grade. He has interviewed Kobe Bryant, Jason Richardson, Earl Boykins, and many other NBA Vets and players. He has even had the opportunity to work out with and get tips from Chauncey Billups himself.

On his journey he has learned a lot from the greats. They not only taught him the physical game, they also taught him the mental game. In this book, he shares some of what he's learned with you! This is the only book out there with input and information from an actual youth player.

You can follow his journey on . . .

Instagram: https://www.instagram.com/moforeal05/

Twitter: https://twitter.com/moforeal05

Troy Horne is a dad who knew nothing about the sport of basketball except that his son wanted to grow up to play the

sport professionally. As a former professional musician, Broadway star, and television actor he had a hypothesis. That hypothesis was that certain truths held fast in all professional industries. He believed that the staples of work hard, master your skills, meet the right people, and put yourself in the right places were not only essential for the music business but essential for all professions. So he went in search of the information that he thought he would need to help his son Moses reach his basketball goals and dreams. Along the way, they ran into the *Mental Toughness Roadblock*.

Mental Toughness For Young Athletes: Eight Proven 5-Minute Mindset Exercises For Kids And Teens Who Play Sports is a collection of exercises that he found to help his young athlete conquer the feelings of nervousness and sports anxiety in high-pressure situations. These exercises come right from talking with Elite college athletes, NBA Veterans and college coaches on their podcast (Hoopchalk Basketball Podcast) have been game-changers in mentally difficult situations. These short but effective mind gym workouts edited just for young athletes have been life-changing when it comes to high performance. See you in the gym!

Sources

Adams, A. (2009). *Seeing Is Believing: The Power of Visualization* Retrieved from https://www.psychologytoday.com/us/blog/flourish/200912/seeing-is-believing-the-power-visualization

Barnett, J. (n.d) *Science Says: Visualization Improves Strength Training* Retrieved from https://breakingmuscle.com/fitness/science-says-visualization-improves-strength-training

Bronkall, N. (2019) *10 Ways to Develop Mental Toughness in Young Athletes* Retrieved from https://www.elitefts.com/education/coaching-education/10-ways-to-develop-mental-toughness-in-young-athletes/

Brown, L. (2017) *15 Critical Secrets Of Mentally Tough People* Retrieved from https://hackspirit.com/15-traits-youre-mentally-tough/

Cohen, B. (2018). *Why Are the NBA's Best Players Getting Better Younger?* Retrieved from https://www.wsj.com/articles/jayson-tatum-nba-youtube-generation-1526483183/

Cohn, P. (n.d) *Mental Toughness Training for Athletes* Retrieved from https://www.peaksports.com/sports-psychology-blog/mental-toughness-training-athletes/

Feinstein, A. (2014). *Why You Should Be Writing Down Your Goals* Retrieved from https://www.forbes.com/sites/ellevate/2014/04/08/why-you-should-be-writing-down-your-goals/#7aa7f9db3397

Gonzalez, K. (2018) *Visualization: 4 Steps To Re-Program Your Mind And Achieve Your Ideal Physique!* Retrieved from https://www.bodybuilding.com/fun/visualization-4-steps-re-program-mind-achieve-ideal-physique.htm

Haden, J. (2014) *7 Habits of People With Remarkable Mental Toughness* Retrieved from https://www.inc.com/jeff-haden/7-habits-of-people-with-remarkable-mental-toughness.html

Haefner, J. (2015). *Mental Rehearsal & Visualization: The Secret to Improving Your Game Without Touching a Basketball!* Retrieved from https://www.breakthroughbasketball.com/mental/visualization.html

James, C. (n.d) *The Science of Developing Mental Toughness in Your Health, Work, and Life* Retrieved from https://jamesclear.com/mental-toughness

Littlewood, Z. (2017) *Mental Muscle Training* Retrieved from https://www.mentalmuscletraining.com/single-post/2016/04/10/5-POWERFUL-EXERCISES-TO-IMPROVE-MENTAL-TOUGHNESS

Mayer, G. (2018) *Subconscious Mind – How to Unlock and Use Its Power* Retrieved from https://thriveglobal.com/stories/subconscious-mind-how-to-unlock-and-use-its-power/

Metivier, A. (2019) *3 Powerful Visualization Exercises [Step-by-Step Walk-Through]* Retrieved from https://www.magneticmemorymethod.com/visualization-exercises/

Morrissey, M. (2017). *The Power of Writing Down Your Goals and Dreams* Retrieved from https://www.huffpost.com/entry/the-power-of-writing-down_b_12002348

Murphy, M. (2018). *Neuroscience Explains Why You Need To Write Down Your Goals If You Actually Want To Achieve Them* Retrieved from https://www.forbes.com/sites/markmurphy/2018/04/15/neuroscience-explains-why-you-need-to-write-down-your-goals-if-you-actually-want-to-achieve-them/#3cf818007905

Operation Meditation (n.d) *3 Key Techniques on How to Train Your Subconscious Mind* Retrieved from http://operationmeditation.com/discover/3-key-techniques-on-how-to-train-your-subconscious-mind/

Polish, J. (2019) *How To Use Visualization In Your Workout, According To A Personal Trainer* Retrieved from https://www.bustle.com/p/how-to-use-visualization-in-your-workout-according-to-a-personal-trainer-18553481

Power Of Positivity (n.d) *10 Things People Do to Become Mentally Tough* Retrieved from https://www.powerofpositivity.com/things-people-do-mentally-tough/

Quinn, E. (2020) *Do Visualization Exercises Help Build Strength?* Retrieved from https://www.verywellfit.com/can-you-build-strength-with-visualization-exercises-3120698

Robertson, C. (2014) *How to Influence Your Subconscious Mind to Achieve Your Goals* Retrieved from http://www.willpowered.co/learn/how-to-influence-the-subconscious-mind

Stone, L. (2016) *The Power of Writing Down Your Goals* Retrieved from https://time.com/4196996/write-down-goals/

Wiest, B. (2018) *13 Ways To Start Training Your Subconscious Mind To Get What You Want* Retrieved from https://www.forbes.com/sites/briannawiest/2018/09/12/13-ways-to-start-training-your-subconscious-mind-to-get-what-you-want/#2c2c2ba7d69f

Made in the USA
Thornton, CO
11/18/24 14:38:58

89a71a64-d378-440a-a4ab-70495308e260R01